A Troll in the House

John Renaud

Copyright © 2022 John Renaud

All rights reserved. No part of this publication may be reproduced, stored in a retrieval system or transmitted in any form or by any means – electronic, mechanical, photocopying, and recording or otherwise – without prior written permission from the author. The exception would be brief passages by a reviewer in a newspaper or magazine or online. To perform any of the above is an infringement of copyright law.

ISBN 978-1-7782010-0-4

Printed and bound In Montreal, QC, Canaada

by Rapido Books

*For Tina, Benjamin & Charlie,
who have to live with the troll too.*

David had a troll in his house. Some people have termites or mice that nest in their home or a raccoon that takes up residence in the attic. Not David, he had a troll.

This troll's name was Tamaru, and he was an ugly little fucker. Tamaru stood just two feet tall. He had a pot belly that surged with each laboured breath above his big, gnarled feet that were trimmed with jagged toenails. His complexion was a washed out grey and ashy colour, darker around his black eyes which made him look punched and beaten. The rest of his face was made of a long pointy nose and even longer, pointy ears. His wiry brown hair grew sparse and messy. Tamaru's discoloured teeth stuck out in random directions, and he smelled badly. Breath, body, it didn't matter, he really stank.

Many years ago, David knew he had a mouse, or more accurately mice, in his house. The tell-tale signs of mangled kitchen garbage and little piles of mouse shit were evident under the kitchen sink. However, trolls are much more subtle than mice, and it took David a long time to know that Tamaru was living in his house.

It all started with the noises. Sometimes David would lay awake at night, struggling to fall asleep. Other times he would stir restlessly, trying to go back to sleep when Tamaru's mischief would unknowingly wake him in the dead of night. He heard whispering noises, like distant echoes, that kept him awake. Back then, David had no idea what sounds a troll makes and Tamaru liked to make noise. He would whisper in low tones that were barely noticeable and left David wondering what he had heard. The noise was so elusive that it didn't always wake up David. Sometimes it just infiltrated his dreams. Pleasant visions of friends, family and good times would take a foul turn, becoming dark and tough to manage. Sometimes he had nightmares.

There were nights when the dreams felt like dark mirrors projecting reflections of his job, and David never liked that. His job was policing. David had been a police officer for more than 20 years. He was a good cop and he liked the work, but he didn't like to bring work home with him. He certainly didn't like to bring work into his dreams.

Years went by as Tamaru grew more and more comfortable living in David's house. Tamaru knew they had a special bond, and he was very attached to David.

Something David truly loved was his garden, and most of all his precious rose. For years he had devoted a lot of care and attention to building a colorful garden filled with interesting variety. He was proud of what he had done, and everyone admired the garden because it was so full and beautiful. David was confident that there was room to grow even more. The potential was endless and that's why he loved to put in the time and effort to tend to every part of the garden, no matter how stretched he felt by the demands.

Tamaru liked David's garden too. However, being a troll, Tamaru had no interest in growing the garden or tending to its needs. It was not in his nature to nurture. Tamaru only wanted a place where he could hang out in comfort. Some place that he could dig around in and get dirty. The best feature of the garden was that it provided great cover. He could hide in there and sneak about practically unseen.

Even though David hadn't seen the troll, he knew something was wrecking his garden. The signs were there. It was getting muddled and some of the colours weren't as bright as they used to be. The time that David put into tending the garden began to drop off because he was so discouraged by his poor results. That demoralized feeling turned into frustration and sometimes anger. David felt like he didn't even know how to garden anymore. Things started to wilt and turn yellow and brown from neglect. This did not go unnoticed, especially not by David's precious, Rose.

David met Rose when they were both just out of college and working their first jobs at an office downtown. They actually worked near each other for a couple of years, but never met, until one day they happened to line up together at the bank. David and Rose were two small town kids who had re-located to the big city and started their adult lives. They hit it off and fell fast in love.

David was a dreamer and Rose loved his creativity and sense of humour. David loved that Rose was practical. He admired her strength, determination, and knack for leadership. They both came from big families where Rose was the oldest in her family and David grew up as the youngest in his.

Soon they were married and started a family of their own. After a while, David felt that being a police officer was the career goal he wanted, and Rose stood by him on that journey. Their family grew and 'The Job' became a big part of the family's life. They worked together on Rose's dreams too. They became a busy family with friends, school connections, kid's sports, church functions, and volunteer commitments. David and Rose had a wonderful garden.

Lately however, Rose could see that the garden wasn't looking like it used to, and she asked David about it. She offered to help him with it and tried to make useful suggestions to turn things around. David was reluctant at first, then the more Rose tried to help, the more defensive he became.

David didn't want to talk about the garden with Rose. He knew he had let things slide a little, but he was determined to fix everything on his own. David was going to pay more attention to tending the garden once again and he started to focus more effort on it. That's when David first saw the troll. He could not believe what he was seeing when he found himself looking eye to eye with Tamaru, and David thought to himself, 'what an ugly little fucker'.

"Hey," said Tamaru.

David just stared back, wide eyes and open mouth. He didn't know how to respond because he was pretty sure he had just gone absolutely insane.

"Hey?" repeated Tamaru. The troll was more than prepared to take his time and wait because he knew he wasn't going anywhere. Besides, trolls don't care. They just don't. The only thing a troll cares about is their bond. Aside from that, they go through their entire lives unabashedly believing "I am what I am, and it is what it is."

David managed to stammer out a greeting. It sounded something like, "mehg?"

Tamaru just twisted his crooked teeth into an awkward smile.

"Screw this." David said, mostly to himself. He shook his head quickly and blinked away the image of the ugly little troll. Then David immersed himself back into tending his garden, with more effort than ever before.

Despite all his labours, David never felt like it was enough. He dove deeper and deeper into being busy. It seemed to David like he just couldn't be still anymore. It wasn't hard to stay busy, there was always lots to do. The fact that he was so disorganized in his tasks made his life seem even busier. David had to back-track a lot. He'd start something, but then get distracted and start something else, then always had to work back around to the other things he had left unfinished. He couldn't always remember if he had done something, or finished what he was supposed to, so the double and triple checking occupied a lot of his busy time too.

All of this activity was making David harder to live with. Though, not for Tamaru. The troll knew that he had settled into a secure spot in David's house. It was Rose who watched with sadness as David's frustration grew and he became distant, short tempered, and angry. She didn't like it and she once again asked David if she could help.

This time he was even more defensive than before because he was certain he was fine and doing what was needed to fix the garden. Besides, how was he ever going to tell Rose there was a troll in the house? She really freaked out that time they found mice in the kitchen. She would completely lose her mind if she knew there was a troll.

So, David set to work on convincing Rose that everything was okay. He told her that she was overreacting. David tried to convince her that the things she was seeing were just her perceptions and not what was really happening. He assured her that he had it all under control.

David knew he had to hide that troll.

As it turns out, trolls have an aversion to alcohol. When David drank, he didn't notice Tamaru nearly as much. Booze was like troll repellent. Just like the subtle discovery of a troll in his house, David made some subtle discoveries about the troll-blocking attributes of liquor.

At first, getting rid of Tamaru on weekends was good. That seemed to help. It made David think 'Why not weekdays, every now and then?' That grew into a few extra days of drinking per week because a few extra days without a troll in your life had to be a good thing. Then a few more days per week. A little experimenting showed David that whisky could push the troll out faster than beer, and with less bloating. David began to feel like he *needed* the drinking because it kept the troll away.

Tamaru wasn't about to be forgotten though. He stomped around in the garden every chance he could, causing chaos and making his presence known. David desperately wanted the garden to be beautiful again. He began to realize that he and the troll shared a strong connection to that garden and for them it was common ground. So, David decided that is where he would confront Tamaru. This time, David was determined they were going to settle their matters once and for all.

"OK," said David. "Just who the hell are you and why are you in my house?"

"I, of course, am Tamaru." Said the troll, who just sat and stared for he was certain no other explanation was needed. Such was the bond he had with David.

"What?!" said David, trying to hide the fear in his almost trembling voice.

"T-a-m-a-r-u." said the troll. More slowly this time, for effect.

David just stared back at the troll with tears welling in his eyes while his thoughts started to run away from him. He began to mumble, "I'm crazy! Nuts...completely lost it. I have really become that person I'd learned to fear all these years. Oh no, oh no, I'm gonna get apprehended; shit, I'll be forced to the hospital! I'm gonna get medicated..."

"Are you alright?" Tamaru asked. Not that he cared. He was a troll and trolls don't care. But someone had to say something. He felt very attached to David, and David looked pretty upset right now.

"Nope! No, I am not alright!" asserted David. "I am confronting a *troll* in my *house,* and this makes no sense to me. I feel like I'm losing my mind." He was angry and venting, but he also feared he was starting to understand something he didn't want to admit. David caught his breath and asked, "Where did you come from?"

Tamaru nodded and obligingly explained. "I was born in a baby's crib. You were there, David, when the baby died. I didn't kill the kid, I swear, she got really sick and that just happens sometimes. I think that's very sad when it does, but the truth of the matter is that's one of the ways us trolls are born. So that is how I came to be. I saw you there and I attached myself to you. It was easy. I just climbed up on your back and you never even noticed really. I went home with you at the end of that shift and ever since, I've grown and lived in your house. It's that simple."

David made his decision then and there. He did not like this ugly little troll. He never asked Tamaru to come home with him and live in his house. He never wanted any of this. David decided he was going to bury Tamaru, and that would be the end of the troll. So, that is what he did.

David took his trusty shovel which had served him well in the garden for so many years. He found a muddy spot in the corner that was shady and lonely and hidden from view to most of the garden. He dug a hole in the cold ground. He had no idea how deep to bury a troll but figured about three feet should do the trick.

Then David walked over to Tamaru with the shovel held menacingly in his hands, fully prepared for a fight. He was more than surprised to find the troll offered no resistance whatsoever. He carried the stout little troll over to the freshly dug hole and dropped him in. Tamaru laid down compliantly because, after all, he didn't care. He curled himself up comfortably and laid still while David covered him back over with dirt and buried him alive.

What David didn't know was that trolls don't stay buried.

Tamaru had followed David home many years ago. He had become quite accustomed to following David everywhere, but he especially liked to be with David at work. Tamaru was there for the fatal collision where David was friends with the family whose little girl died. He was there for all those suicide calls and sudden deaths. Tamaru was there with David every time for what seemed like an endless series of death notifications to the next of kin. Those were the ones that Tamaru remembered so well because they were always unpredictable and volatile. He was there too when that little girl was stabbed by her father. David really fell apart after that one and Tamaru was almost certain David had seen him that morning, sitting right there in the cruiser beside him, though David's vision was probably blurry from all the tears.

Tamaru knew the strength of their bond, even if David didn't understand it yet. He lived in David's house, and he was determined to prove their connection. That was the only thing Tamaru ever cared about in his whole troll life. He would not let a little thing like getting buried stand in his way. Tamaru began making the garden decay. From his damp, dark corner, he was able to reach out and begin choking the very roots of all the things David loved and cared for.

The garden was falling apart faster than ever before, rotting from below and turning barren. Like stones in a frost cycle, Tamaru worked his way back up to the surface and was up to his old tricks of stumping around in the garden. He was louder now, almost demanding to be heard. He blatantly knocked things over and smashed anything he could. The damage was becoming really obvious. David always found himself making excuses to Rose about the growing disarray of the garden.

Until the day Rose had had enough of watching the garden fall to ruin. She confronted David, and with all the love and caring affection she could muster, she gently asked, "What the fuck is wrong with you?"

David felt that he had no defence left. He had no more ammunition to fight with and nothing else to hide behind. All he had left was the truth and the time had come to tell it. It was like a dam broke when the tears flowed. David told Rose all about Tamaru. He had finally found the courage to tell her there was a troll in the house.

That was when Rose blew his mind. She said, "I know."

David stood there in disbelief. "How?" he whispered.

"A little while ago, I began to suspect that a troll was behind all of this trouble." In fact, Rose had been suspicious about the troll for years. She had felt Tamaru's effect on David. The times when he came home from work, sad or hurting, and he'd tell her a little bit about a bad call he'd been on – Rose felt Tamaru's presence. It was like the troll had changed the temperature and made things colder then changed the colours and made them all dull and grey.

Rose continued, "Once you started to tell me about him today, he just stepped out into the light, and I could see him." She added, "He's an ugly little fucker."

David confided, "I don't know what to do."

Rose thought for a moment, then said, "Exterminator. Like, when we had mice in the house. You just need to find an exterminator who handles trolls then ask them for help."

It seemed like a plan to David, and he felt a great sense of relief. For the next few hours David and Rose had the most open and honest conversation of their lives. Rose was able to tell David how helpless she felt when he rejected her suggestions. She told him she felt foolish and doubted herself when David would tell her that everything was fine, and she was just seeing what she wanted to see. That hurt because Rose never wanted to see David struggle with the garden.

They came to a much better understanding of how each of them felt and what they believed would help going forward. All the while, Tamaru just sat quietly in the corner. He was still there when they locked up, turned off the lights and said 'good night' to this emotional day. Tamaru wasn't going anywhere.

The next day, David started his research. He thought of a few close friends he could trust with the news of the troll. Experience told him to keep the circle tight because, once people find out you have a troll in your house, they might treat you differently. David was worried people would feel they couldn't rely on him now. He assumed that if anyone at work knew about Tamaru, he'd be in trouble. He was afraid that he would be restricted to some kind of special duties, and no one would trust him to do real police work anymore.

Luckily, there was one friend who David was certain could help. Gillian was someone who actually had a little experience with trolls and other similar creatures. Sure enough, she recommended a few exterminators who she believed could absolutely help with Tamaru. A short list of professionals who specialized in trolls. Gillian was truly supportive with David and praised him for deciding to deal with the troll. She assured David that he would not regret getting professional help.

David did a little more research on the options Gillian had told him about and he eventually chose one from her list. This exterminator had a website that he could search through to read about her methods and approach, which seemed to David like a good fit for his troll problem. David reached out by email and arranged an appointment with the exterminator, Dr Katherine McCallister, PhD.

On Friday of that week, more than five years after Tamaru the troll had moved into his house, David walked into that exterminator's office and said, "I need help."

"Call me Katherine," said the exterminator and she motioned for David to take a seat on the office couch.

David noticed the room was neat and clean and the couch was comfortable. One wall was decorated with several nicely framed scrolls and degrees. 'Exterminator School?' wondered David. The office was very professional but also snug and peaceful. He felt nervous, but calm.

Katherine stated, "I know we have had a few emails, but maybe you could start by telling me a little bit more about why you're here today."

"Well, I don't have a troll in my house," were the next brilliant words out of David's mouth. 'Stupid', he thought to himself. David followed his ridiculous opening statement with some background on his family and his job history. He added more and more information about his work experiences – especially the tough ones – then he moved on to describing his garden in great detail. That lead to explaining how broken his garden had become, particularly in the last year or so, and the trouble that was creating for him and Rose. He managed to describe a lot of elements about having a troll in his house without ever actually admitting that he had one.

David paused to wipe his tearing eyes. He felt exposed, emotional, and a little embarrassed.

Katherine was gentle and direct when she said, "David, you have a troll in your house."

"Are you sure?" asked David.

"Oh yes, I'm sure. I can see him sitting right there beside you on the couch," she said, "and he's an ugly little fucker."

Tamaru was getting rather accustomed to that descriptor and, well, he didn't care.

"Hi." said Tamaru to the exterminator.

"Hello," replied Katherine. "I wonder, do you have a name?"

"Why yes, I am Tamaru," said the troll.

"I'm sure you are," she knowingly replied. "What are we going to do with you, Tamaru?" Katherine asked, rhetorically.

Tamaru must have caught her meaning because he just sat there sporting his crooked smile and he offered no suggestions.

Katherine assured David that he shouldn't worry too much and that she could help him with the troll. That news brought him a great deal of relief.

David, with Tamaru in tow, came back to Katherine's office for more appointments. After a few sessions, Katherine had made a plan and determined that it was time to put Tamaru to work.

"David, we are going to send Tamaru on an adventure," said Katherine as David settled in for today's hour-long talk.

David listened closely while Katherine explained. "Tamaru will go back to some of the traumatic events that he shared with you; the times and places where your bond was formed. When he travels back on this journey, he will visit all of those sad and scattered memories. Tamaru will look at things differently this time, search for a new perspective, and process those memories in a way that will allow you to keep them safely stored but accessible. I think that when his work is done, you'll be able to turn all of those experiences into just another part of your wonderful garden."

David was happy to know this little troll was going to be put to work after years of rent-free living in his house. "This ought to make up for the damage he did while screwing up my garden."

With those instructions reinforced and repeated back by the little troll, Katherine was confident he understood what to do. They sent Tamaru out the door and on his way.

Tamaru was pleased for the chance to protect his bond with David. He cared about their bond because Tamaru recognised that he was safe in David's house. It doesn't always work out that way for a troll. No, sometimes trolls live in a house where things just spin way too far and go out of control. When that happens, the host can set their own house on fire and burn it to the ground. That's very bad news for the troll as the bond is consumed and they are rendered homeless and lost. Sometimes they can latch onto one of the loved ones left behind. Usually though, there is so much confusion and pain in the wake of a tragic loss that the troll just bears the brunt of everyone's blame then fades away into obscurity. That troll is left alone and forgotten.

Tamaru knew there was a lot of time and distance that he needed to cover. He went back and forth, all across the big city that he once patrolled with David. Tamaru became a time traveller moving back through the years on his quest to find the worst of David's trauma scenes. He spent a lot of time journaling about his adventures, writing detailed and emotional narratives that told the story of those incidents he and David had attended. Tamaru found himself chasing a swirl of memories, like scattered photographs caught up in a tornado. He captured all of these and started to archive the images and put them into an organized system.

Everywhere that Tamaru went, he slowed things down and took his time. He stood back and looked at the big picture. Sometimes he changed where he stood, then moved again, always in search of a fresh perspective. Tamaru stood on higher ground where he was able to consider the totality of every situation. He could look beyond the worst, and very specific elements of any event to find some good in each story – even in the tragic ones.

Whenever he did this, Tamaru found himself able to see the points where David was stuck. He found an understanding in the things David felt badly about, could not forget, and seemed to struggle moving past. He allowed himself to feel the emotions behind the stories and really think about what was causing them.

All along the way, Tamaru collected many treasures to bring back for David.

Months went by before Tamaru returned from his mission. He met up with David in Katherine's office. He was dragging an ornate and heavy wooden chest. It looked like a weathered antique that could have fallen off a pirate ship centuries ago.

David couldn't help but notice that Tamaru wasn't such an ugly little fucker anymore. He was still a troll, possessed of all those less than desirable troll features, but he somehow looked restored. His grey skin had a more even colour and brighter tone. His messy hair was now neatly combed. Even his teeth had straightened out and looked to be about three shades whiter. Most of all, Tamaru didn't really stink anymore and that was a welcome relief.

"I worked really hard while I was out on my adventure, David," Tamaru started excitedly. "I believe that you and Katherine will be pleased with the treasures that I have brought back with me." as he motioned dramatically towards the heavy chest in the middle of the office floor.

"Go ahead Tamaru," Katherine encouraged, "share."

With a broad smile on his face, Tamaru opened the chest. He reached deep inside and the first thing he pulled out was a bouquet of flowers. They were lovely and colourful and instantly reminded David of his own garden.

"These," said Tamaru, "I found in a pretty little garden outside of that apartment building."

David asked, "What apartment building?"

"You already know."

"Where the baby died?"

"That's right, David. Where she died. Where I was born. That was a tragic and terrible call. You did the very best you could. You responded so fast and got there first. You did CPR in a scene that was filled with chaos. Those other officers who came, the EMS team, the hospital staff – no one ever gave up on her. There was just nothing that could have saved her. Through all the pain and emotion, you were the professional helper the family needed in that awful moment. You and your friends gave comfort, and safety to a family on the worst day of their lives."

"So, these flowers are a good thing from a sad place," Tamaru continued. "I'm giving you this treasure so that you'll remember to drop the mental filter which only lets you see the bad parts of an event. Then you can also see the genuine good that was done."

He reached back into the beat-up old chest and both feet lifted off the floor as he grunted and struggled to retrieve a substantial rock. It took all his effort and both hands to hold it steady. "This," Tamaru groaned, "is really heavy!" and he struggled to avoid his massive feet as he plunked it down on the floor.

"As I was saying, this is a rock. I found it against a curb in the parking lot at the hospital. The same hospital where your friend's grand daughter died in the crash. I have brought this for you David because you have been the rock to so many at the hospital. All those unstable people suffering terribly with their mental health when you brought them to the hospital for help. You were their rock when they had no stability of their own. All those families you sat with at the hospital, so deep in their grief and not knowing what the next step would be. You were the rock they could lean on."

David was really starting to see Tamaru differently now. A change in perspective created a whole new understanding of the trauma experience. For the first time, David could truly feel their bond and he knew that he didn't want to fight that anymore.

Tamaru continued under Katherine's watchful eye. He rummaged around in the cavernous chest once again, then pulled out a glass of cold water.

"David, do you remember all those death notifications, where you had to sit and talk to the next of kin?"

"Of course, I do."

"And remember how you didn't like doing them, and sometimes it just got so emotional and seemed to go totally off the rails?"

"Yes. I sure do"

"Well, do you remember how you handled that? How you used to calm folks and settle them down and bring them back to listening, at least a little bit?"

"Yeah, I used to get them a glass of water."

"Those were wicked calls David. Even I used to cringe when we got dispatched to them because I knew you were about to take another hit. You should remember, with this glass of water, that even in the face of pain, and yelling, and venting emotions, you showed compassion. When loved ones would wail through denial, anger, bargaining, depression and acceptance you stood by with patience and kindness. In sudden tragedy, you were the person that they needed at that very moment."

David let a little smile show as he was enjoying seeing this new point of view that Tamaru had.

While David considered these alternative thoughts, Tamaru dove back into the chest and pulled out a hefty, leather-bound photo album. He told David about all the swirling images that he found as he travelled across space and time, re-visiting their sad and terrible events.

"It was really hard to keep them all straight," he explained. "They were all out of order and flapping around and flying about like leaves blowing in the wind. So, I grabbed a bunch of them," said Tamaru, miming his actions, jumping and snatching at the air around his head, "and I stuffed them in my pockets. Then I stuffed more in my pockets, until they were full. Once I had a handle on them, I got them organized and placed in the right order. Then I decided to put them in this book."

Tamaru presented the album to David who started to flip through the pages. David noted with a heavy heart that it was filled with sad memories, but he realized he could deal with looking at them now.

Then something odd began to happen. Tamaru did not reach back into his treasure chest. Instead, he closed the heavy lid then scrambled up clumsily to stand on top of the box. He looked at Katherine and back at David as he forcefully, and obnoxiously, cleared his throat. Tamaru was about to spit out whatever his unclogging had just generated, but Katherine's raised eyebrow made him change his mind.

"Pardon me," he said apologetically.

Then, to everyone's amazement, Tamaru began to sing.

He sang with the most unbelievable voice! It was like a whole flock of colourful songbirds had learned an opera. The song was moving and sad but cheerful too and so filled with emotion, depth, and vibrato. Tamaru's voice soared through a wide range from tender soprano to dynamic baritone. When he finished his song, Tamaru gave an exaggerated bow. Katherine and David offered up their applause for the beautiful music.

David stammered, "That was amazing Tamaru."

"That," the troll said, "was the final treasure I have for you. It is my own gift to you David for all the work you have done to comprehend and heal from your trauma. Healing is a process and it only started when you finally found the courage to *talk* about it. At long last, you gave your trauma a voice, and I thank you."

The afternoon sun was filtering into the window of Katherine's office, warming the comfortable space. David looked at Tamaru who had curled himself up on the couch to nap in the sunbeam, and suddenly he wondered, 'now what?'

"Katherine," he said, "what do I do with Tamaru now? All this time, I thought you were going to exterminate him?"

"I'm not that kind of exterminator," she explained. "I'm the kind that helps you to catch the creature, then helps you tame him. Tamaru is part of your life David, but I believe now you can live with him, in peace."

David understood and he knew she was right. He motioned for Tamaru and the little troll happily climbed up onto David's back. It took one quick adjustment, but then David felt pretty comfortable. "I guess we're on our way then, Katherine. Thank you for all your help."

"You're welcome. Check in with me every now and then, okay?"

"I will," promised David as he walked out of the office.

"Let's head home," said David. "We can tell Rose the good news, then we'll find you a safe spot of your own in the garden."

John Renaud is a military veteran and police officer who lives in Ilderton, ON. After spending several years undiagnosed and untreated, John sought out professional psychological help to deal with his trauma injury. The ongoing efforts of therapy and support from his family and friends have created the circumstances that allow him to live with PTSD.

www.ingramcontent.com/pod-product-compliance
Lightning Source LLC
Chambersburg PA
CBHW070343120526
44590CB00017B/2990